LEIF ERIKSON
THE LUCKY

LEIF ERIKSON THE LUCKY

MALCOLM C. JENSEN

A Visual Biography

*Illustrated with authentic prints
and documents*

*Franklin Watts
New York / London / 1979*

Maps by Vantage Art, Inc.
Photo research by Selma Friedman
Cover design by Rafael Hernandez

Library of Congress Cataloging in Publication Data

Jensen, Malcolm C
    Leif Erikson the Lucky.

    (A Visual biography)
    Bibliography: p.
    Includes index.
    SUMMARY: A biography of Leif Erikson describing his boyhood in Iceland, his father Erik the Red's voyage to Greenland, and his own voyage to North America around 1000 A.D.
    1. America—Discovery and exploration—Norse—Juvenile literature.   2. Vikings—Juvenile literature. 3. Leiv Eiriksson, d. ca. 1020—Juvenile literature. 4. Explorers—Iceland—Biography—Juvenile literature. 5. Explorers—America—Biography—Juvenile literature. [1. Ericson, Leif, d. ca. 1020. 2. Explorers. 3. America—Discovery and exploration—Norse]   I. Title.
E105.J46   970.01'3'0924 [B]   78-11181
ISBN 0-531-02297-8

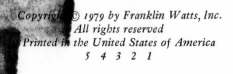

For the High One

A Note on the Illustrations

Many of the illustrations in this book show reconstructions of actual Viking ships, homes, and churches excavated in Norway and in Viking settlements in the New World. Also shown are reconstructions of their weapons and navigational instruments. Great interest in the adventures of these bold explorers has led to much romantic exaggeration in depicting them, and we have included many such drawings, as well as excerpts from early written references to the Vikings.

Illustrations credits:

New York Public Library Picture Collection:
pp. 2 (top), 10, 14 (bottom), 19, 22, 44, and 47.

Illustrated London News: p. 2 (bottom).

Nationalmuseet, Copenhagen: p. 5 (bottom right).

Metropolitan Museum of Art. Rogers Fund, 1956:
p. 5 (bottom left).

Universitetets Oldsaksamling, Oslo:
pp. 5 (top) and 9 (bottom left and right).

Culver Pictures, Inc.: frontispiece,
pp. 14 (top), 17 (top), 27, 37, and 38.

Aftenposten: p. 17 (bottom).

Norwegian Information Service in the United States:
pp. 9 (top left), 20 and 34.

The Bettmann Archive: p. 29.

British Museum: p. 9 (top right).

The Icelandic Tourist Office: p. 53.

LEIF THE LUCKY

Leif Erikson the Lucky was born sometime after A.D. 960 in Iceland. Sometime before A.D. 1025, he died, probably in Greenland.

In the year 1000 or 1001, Leif did something that has caused his name to be remembered for almost a thousand years. He explored and named parts of North America. He even built houses there, almost five hundred years before Christopher Columbus sailed to America.

In this book, you will read how Leif got the nickname "the Lucky." But you will also see that his life was touched by strangeness and evil, and that there are mysteries about him that linger to this day. You will have to decide for yourself about the luck of Leif Erikson.

Erik the Red, as an Icelandic
artist of the 1600s imagined him.
Below: a reconstruction of the main
hall of a Viking house where a force
of fighting men, such as Erik the
Red kept, might have been housed.

GROWING UP
IN ICELAND

Leif's father was called Erik the Red, because he had red hair and a red beard. Erik came to Iceland in about A.D. 960. He was about fifteen then and had already been involved in some killings in Norway. Erik and his father—Leif's grandfather—had had to leave Norway because of these killings.

Some years after Erik the Red arrived in Iceland, he married a woman named Thjodhild and moved to Haukadale, in the western part of the country. It is probably there that Leif was born. Leif's mother was a member of a fairly important, well-to-do Icelandic family. She was as tough and stubborn as her husband.

During the fifteen years or so that Erik and Thjodhild lived as husband and wife in Iceland, they were forced to move several times as a result of fights Erik had with his neighbors. In one fight, Erik killed two men. Later, he fought a battle with another family in which several men died. After this battle, Leif's father kept a force of fighting men on his farm.

Iceland—a cool, wet land of glaciers, volcanoes, and earthquakes—had been settled mainly by people from Norway. In Erik's time, people from Norway and the other Scandinavian countries were known as the Norse, Northmen, or Vikings.

Prosperous Icelandic families such as Erik's lived together in long, narrow farmhouses. Such houses were usually about 40 feet (12 m) long by about 12 feet (3.5 m) wide. The walls were set low in the earth and were made of stone and turf. The roofs were rounded and made of driftwood covered with grassy earth. From a distance, such houses looked like low hills. Inside, a long trench held a charcoal-burning fire. Along both walls were earthen benches about 3 feet (.9 m) wide. The benches had wooden seats, often covered with furs or blankets, and were used for sitting and sleeping.

As a boy, Leif would have shared in many of the tasks that made up everyday life in Iceland: raising cattle, sheep, and horses; fishing; hunting wildfowl; and gathering driftwood. And, because he was the son of Erik the Red, Leif would also have heard much talk of weapons—the long, double-edged Viking sword, the spear for throwing or thrusting, and the Viking battle-ax. Leif would have heard how to care for such weapons, how to use them, and what it felt like to kill a man with them.

Icelanders were generally law-abiding people. They had public lawmaking assemblies or courts called *Things*, where all people who were not thralls—slaves—had a right to gather, speak, and settle disputes according to Icelandic laws. But not all these laws were the same as ours today.

For example, killing a person was a serious matter in Iceland, but Icelandic laws about killing were different in several ways from our own. First, Icelandic law accepted as valid many more reasons for killing than our laws do today. In the Iceland of Erik's time, a man could rightfully be killed for deliberately saying something insulting to another. The theory behind that was that a person should keep a civil tongue in his head when speaking to an armed, proud Icelandic farmer, or be prepared to pay the consequences.

Second, it was up to Icelandic families to enforce the laws. Today, most countries have a police force that arrests people who are suspected of wrongdoing, a court system that decides guilt or

Below left: a Viking sword hilt, inlaid with silver and copper. Below right: a Viking battle-ax, also inlaid with metals. Left: a true Viking helmet. The winged or horned helmets so often seen in artists' drawings of the period were pure fiction, invented mostly by nineteenth-century romantic writers.

innocence and sets the punishment, and another system that carries out the punishment through fines, imprisonment, or execution. The Icelanders had only the court system—the Things. Icelandic families had to carry out the policing and punishing functions themselves.

Another difference was that sometimes a killing could be settled by the payment of a fine, or blood-money. A Thing could suggest that the killer's family pay a fine to the victim's family and might also suggest an amount, which depended on how valuable a person the victim was. If the amount of blood-money was acceptable to both families, and was paid, the matter was then legally settled. All members of the killer's family—even very distant relatives such as fourth cousins—were expected to chip in to pay the blood-money amount, and all members of the victim's family benefited from this payment. But it was up to the victim's family to make sure that the blood-money was paid.

However, the victim's family could also decide that it would not accept blood-money, however large the sum. It could instead decide that the killer, or some member of the killer's family, had to die in order for justice to be done. If such a decision was reached, then the victim's family had to seek its own vengeance and do its own killing. Sometimes two large families might seek vengeance from each other again and again, leading to blood-feuds that could last for many years. While Leif was growing up, his father was involved in at least two blood-feuds.

Sometimes a Thing would decide to banish someone involved in a blood-feud. This meant that the Thing took away from this person, for a certain amount of time, the protection of the laws that governed killing. A banished person thus became an "outlaw," and anybody had the right to kill such an outlaw without fear of having to pay a fine or having to answer to the outlaw's family. The banished person didn't *have* to leave home, but the chances of staying alive while under banishment were not good. Most Icelanders who were banished therefore went into hiding or tried to get away from Iceland entirely. While Leif was growing up, his father was banished twice.

This system of justice may seem cruel or stupid to most people today. But to the Icelanders of the time it seemed sensible. Some people, they believed, just plain deserved killing. It also seemed right that those who were grieved or harmed by a person's death should get something in return—either blood-money or vengeance. To Icelanders, killing was not necessarily bad. What was a crime—an unthinkable, unforgivable crime—was to kill someone *in secret*, and not announce right away what you had done and why. If a killing was secret, nobody could decide what was right, and justice could not be done.

As Leif was growing up, he must have heard the Icelandic laws about killing discussed many times. It was by no means every Icelandic boy whose father and grandfather had been involved in killings, blood-feuds, and banishment.

It is interesting, therefore, that Leif Erikson, born into a hot-tempered, warlike family, seems to have committed only one act of violence in his life. A few years before his death, Leif tortured three men. He did this in order to find out if his sister had indeed secretly murdered thirty-five people.

TO GREENLAND

In the early 980s, Leif's father, Erik, was banished from Iceland for three years.

Fifty years earlier, a sailor on his way to Iceland had been blown off course and had reported seeing skerries, or little islands, off in the west somewhere. Erik decided to spend the period of his banishment checking this story out. So he sailed westward from Iceland and found, not skerries, but the largest island in the world. Erik named this island Greenland, and so it has been called ever since.

The ship Erik used was not the long, low, dragonlike Viking warship that had so terrorized Western Europe for almost two centuries. The deep-sea ship that the Northmen used for trading and for traveling in the North Atlantic was called a *knörr*. The knörr looked somewhat like the Viking dragonship, but was wider, deeper, and usually shorter. About 60 feet (18 m) long, the knörr had plank decks in front and back and a large open hold for carrying cargo, including cattle and horses. A knörr usually had one small boat on board, and it often towed a second boat. Like the dragonship, the knörr had a large steering oar near the stern. Unlike the dragonship, however, the knörr was almost entirely sail-powered and had only a few oar holes for rowing. Under very favorable sailing conditions, the knörr could travel more than 10 miles (16 km) an hour. It was the most seaworthy ship of its time.

Above left: the reconstructed Oseberg ship, so-called because it was excavated near the Oseberg farm in Norway in 1904. This Viking ship was probably not used for long voyages. It was too low and too frail. However, it probably was used for traveling along the quieter seacoasts. Above right: an elaborately carved wooden headpost of a Viking dragonship built around A.D. 800. Below left: The reconstructed Gokstad ship, found on the Gokstad farm in Norway in 1880. This ship probably was used for sailing in open seas. Below right: These small boats, found with the Gokstad ship, probably accompanied it.

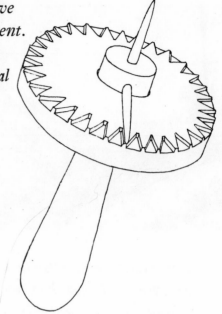

A reconstruction of what might have been a Viking navigational instrument. Shadows cast by the vertical pin could indicate north. The horizontal pin could be a course indicator.

The Norse seagoers of Erik's time had no compasses, no maps or charts, and no way of accurately figuring how far east or west they had sailed. But they were able to sail directly from Bergen, Norway, to Erik's colony in Greenland—a voyage of more than 1,800 miles (2,900 km)—in about twelve days and nights. How did they do it?

Viking navigators had some way of gauging latitude fairly accurately. They could tell, within a degree or so—about 69 miles (110 km)—how far north or south of any given parallel, or line of latitude, they were. The Norse shipmasters may have had a kind of portable sundial, or perhaps a crystal-like stone that could show them where the sun was even through a fog-shrouded sky. In any case, the Vikings used the position of the sun and stars to sail, with little error, along a given parallel.

Furthermore, the Viking seafarers observed and remembered even the tiniest details about the sea. The color and temperature of the water, the shape of the waves, the nature and direction of drifting wood, the flight paths of birds—all told the Norse sailors something about where they were heading.

North Atlantic seagoers sometimes used ravens as a way of locating their position. They would release a raven and watch it. If the bird flew up, circled around, and then flew back down to the mast, the sailors knew that no land was near. If the bird flew back in the direction from which the ship had come, the sailors knew that they weren't yet halfway to their destination. If the bird flew in the direction the ship was headed, the Vikings knew that their destination must be fairly near.

Of course, when sailing between two known points, Norse seafarers would know in advance how much time the voyage should take. They would also be on the lookout for landmarks that would tell them if they were headed on the right course. If they were sailing from Norway to Iceland, for example, they knew that the voyage should take them seven days. In two days they should be able to glimpse the Shetland Islands to the south, and in four days they should be able to see in the distance to the north certain high parts of the Faroe Islands.

Erik the Red had such sea-knowledge. If a man was rich enough to own a ship in those days, he also knew how to sail it. He was expected to stand at the steering oar, and the lives of the people on board were his responsibility.

Erik probably took about thirty men with him on his search for new land to the west. We don't know if he took the young Leif with him, but several factors suggest that he might have. First, there was the family tradition. The teen-aged Erik went with his father into banishment, and so it is likely that Erik took his teen-aged son with him. Second, as a boy in his mid-teens, Leif would be considered nearly an adult. Third, Erik would have wanted to give his son Leif all the experience of command and seamanship he could.

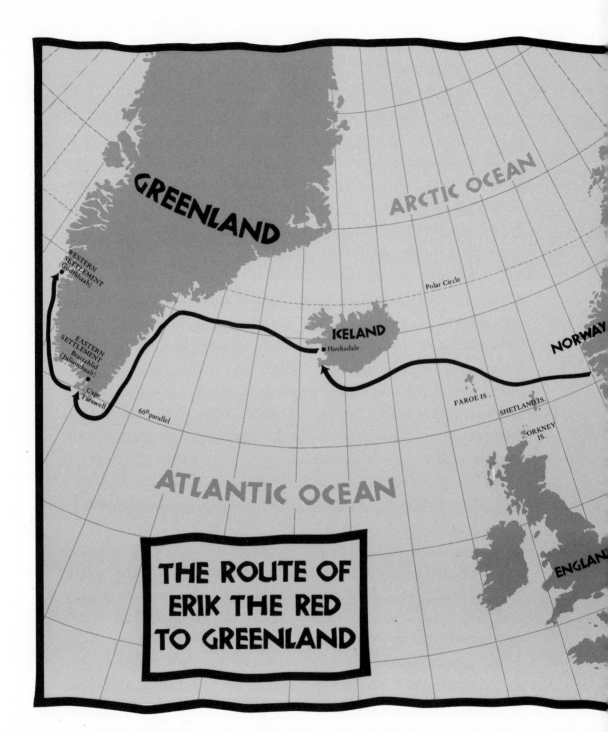

GREENLAND

ARCTIC OCEAN

WESTERN
SETTLEMENT
(Godthhaab)

Polar Circle

ICELAND

NORWAY

Haukadale

EASTERN
SETTLEMENT
Brattahlid
(Julianehaab)

Cape
Farewell

60° parallel

FAROE IS.

SHETLAND IS.

ORKNEY
IS.

ATLANTIC OCEAN

ENGLAND

THE ROUTE OF
ERIK THE RED
TO GREENLAND

Finally, there is little doubt that Leif became an experienced deep-sea sailor at some point. He is said to have made at least one round-trip voyage from Greenland to Norway. Later, we are given a glimpse of Leif at the steering oar, alert, sharp-eyed, shaving things close. Leif must have learned to handle a knörr early in his life, and he is more likely to have learned this by sailing with Erik than by hiding in Iceland.

When Erik sailed away from Iceland, he could look back and see a large glacier looming behind him as a landmark. Four days and nights later, on the 65° north parallel, Erik spied another towering glacier. This one was on the east coast of Greenland. These two glaciers were to form part of the standard Iceland-to-Greenland sailing directions for the next 350 years.

The east coast of Greenland was, and still is, a nightmare of rock and ice cliffs. But Erik sailed southwest along this coast, rounded Cape Farewell, and then came upon a Northman's paradise.

Today, many people think that Greenland is an odd name for an island that is mainly one huge slab of ice. But Greenland is permanently covered with a glacier not because it is so cold but because it is so high—reaching more than 10,000 feet (3,048 m) above sea level. The sea-level coastal areas on the southwestern side of Greenland are not wastelands.

Look at a globe or a map showing the north polar regions. Follow the 60° north parallel. You will see that this parallel passes through or near several cities: Leningrad in the Soviet Union, Stockholm in Sweden, Oslo in Norway, and Anchorage in Alaska. You will see, too, that this parallel passes near Julianehaab, Greenland.

It was in the Julianehaab area that Erik made his first explorations. It was there that Erik later built his home-farm, called Brattahlid. It was there too that the Norse established a Christian European community that was to last almost 500 years.

Above: an artist's view of Erik arriving in the Greenland area. Right: a view of Tunigdliarfik, once known as Erik's Fjord, in Greenland.

The southwestern coast of Greenland, which Erik first saw in summer, must have caused his Northman's heart to leap. Hundreds of small islands were there, teeming with birds. And where seabirds abound, so do fish. Deep, familiar-looking fjords were there—safe, sheltered harbors for the farmer-fisherman. And back in the fjords, nestled against the steeply rising mountains, were bright green pasturelands, for which the stock-raising Norse hungered above all else. There were even trees there—willow, birch, juniper. They weren't very big trees, at most 20 feet (6 m) tall and a few inches (cm) thick. But to Erik and his crew, coming from a now almost treeless Iceland, such trees seemed a forest.

Even today, when Greenland is a few degrees colder than it was in Leif's time, the southwestern coastal regions are very pleasant in the summer. In June, days there are about as mild as an early spring day in New England. And winters in southwestern Greenland are not usually as cold as winters in North Dakota or northern Minnesota.

For three years, Erik explored the west coast of Greenland, from what is now Julianehaab to what is now Godthaab. He didn't lose a man, partly because he was a fine leader and partly because the new land offered plenty of food—fish, birds, birds' eggs, berries, walrus, bear, and seal. Erik's safety record was also the result of a happy coincidence: this new green land was uninhabited.

GREENLAND
AND BEYOND

In the winter of 984 or 985, Erik's period of banishment was over, and he and his men returned to Iceland.

Erik told the Icelanders about Greenland. Things were now not good in Iceland. There had been a famine. The pastureland was overgrazed, and almost all the trees had been cut down. So the Icelanders listened when Erik told them about this new land to the west. In fact, their reaction may have been a little too enthusiastic for Erik's liking. Erik wanted elbowroom in Greenland. He may have grown worried that too many people would come to Greenland, because he started saying that Greenland was just a nice-sounding name he had made up in order to get people to go there.

The following summer, twenty-five ships sailed from Iceland for Greenland. They probably carried about 750 men, women, and children. But only fourteen ships made it. The rest were sunk, or driven back to Iceland by a great storm. Greenland was settled by about 400 people. Among these first settlers were Erik, Thjodhild, and their son Leif.

The home-farm established by Erik at Brattahlid lay some 60 miles (97 km) inland from the coast, at the head of a fjord. The great hall, or main room, of the Brattahlid house measured more than 12 feet (3.5 m) wide by 45 feet (13.5 m) long. A small stream, covered with flat stones, ran through it. The walls, mainly of stone, were 6 feet (1.8 m) thick in places. The door faced west and gave a view of the fjord.

Left: Erik relating his
Greenland adventures
to fellow Icelanders.
Below: the excavation
site of Erik and
Leif's Brattahlid.

Later, other buildings were added to the main hall—a room with a great fireplace in the floor, a separate sleeping room, store-rooms, and a room in which a well was dug. The lovely, dark green pastures around Brattahlid supported forty cattle, as well as horses, sheep, goats, and a few pigs. There were four barns. The entire farm was sheltered by low hills.

Eventually, the newly settled area contained about 190 Norse farms, and was known as the Eastern Settlement, to distinguish it from the smaller Western Settlement, which had about 90 farms. The Western Settlement was in what is now the Godthaab area, about 400 miles (640 km) to the north and west of Erik's colony.

By the 1200s, the Eastern Settlement had a stone cathedral, Gardar, where the bishop of Greenland lived. It also had a Benedictine monastery, an Augustine nunnery, and twelve churches. At its peak, the Norse population in Greenland was at least 3,000, and may have reached twice that number.

The Eastern Settlement seems to have prospered from the start. Erik the Red was its law speaker. In Iceland, it was the duty of the law speaker to memorize all the laws, and to recite one third of them at each yearly meeting of the Thing. We are not sure if Erik did this, because we are not sure how or if the Greenland colony differed in its customs from Iceland. But we do know that Greenland had its own laws, its own Thing, and that the law speaker always lived at Brattahlid. After his father's death, Leif became the law speaker and leader of the Eastern Settlement.

In most respects, Greenland was self-supporting. However, there was not enough wood for shipbuilding, house-building, and fuel. Greenland also lacked sufficient iron for making tools. Grains for making porridge, bread, and beer were hard to grow. Since Iceland was also poor in timber, iron, and grains, these things had to be imported from Norway. In return, the Greenlanders shipped to Norway several trade items that were prized there—walrus and

The excavation site of a Norse church
probably built around A.D. *1100 in*
what was the Western Settlement.

narwhal ivory, furs, woolens, enormously strong ropes of braided walrus hide, and live polar bears. Greenland's most valuable export, however, was a vicious white bird called a gyrfalcon, native only to Greenland and arctic North America. European monarchs treasured this bird because it was the finest hunting falcon in the world.

Erik and the other settlers had much to do that first summer. They spread out over a hundred miles (160 km) of coastline, staking out homesteads and pastureland. Then came the job of house-building and barn-building. Nobody had much time to wonder about other new lands elsewhere. Even in those first hectic months, however, some Greenlanders must have guessed that there was land to the west of them. Birds were flying in from somewhere, across what is now called the Davis Strait. On very clear days, cloud formations indicating land could be glimpsed to the west from high on the Greenland mountains. There were signs that some non-European people had at one time lived in Greenland,

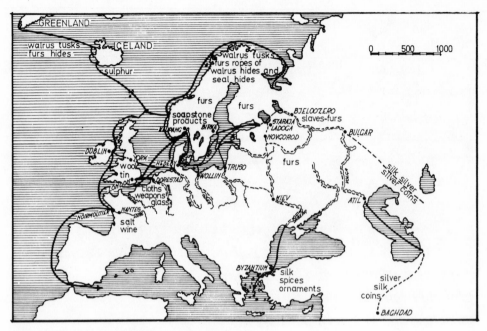

The principal trading routes of
the Vikings (distance in kilometers).

and these people must have gone somewhere. As it happened, however, late that first summer, Greenlanders were told about land in
the west by someone who had seen it.

Bjarni Herjolfson was a young trader-farmer from Iceland.
He had sailed from Norway to Iceland, intending to spend the
winter at his father's home, as was his custom. When Bjarni got
to Iceland, he learned that his father and all the family had packed
up and gone off to Greenland with Erik. Bjarni was a very single-
minded fellow. He didn't even bother to unload his ship when he
heard the news. Instead, he just took right off for Greenland.

Three days out from Iceland, Bjarni's ship was blown south
by strong winds. For many days, the sea was blanketed by a thick
fog, and the crew could not get their bearings. Then the sun came
out, and Bjarni headed west. A day later, the crew saw a land with
low hills and trees.

"Whatever this land is, it is not Greenland," Bjarni said. "Greenland is supposed to have glaciers."

Then they sailed north for two days and sighted land once again—this time a flat land with some trees.

Bjarni knew this wasn't Greenland, and he refused to stop.

Bjarni then sailed north and east for another three days and saw land once more. This time the land was high, rocky, and covered with glaciers. Bjarni wouldn't stop here, either. "This country is worthless," he said.

Bjarni kept sailing in a northeast direction, but then was blown southward in a gale. After four days, Bjarni and his crew spotted more land.

"This looks like the place," said Bjarni. "It fits what I have been told about Greenland. Head in toward the land."

A small boat lay beached on the cape where the ship landed. Bjarni's father lived nearby. Bjarni was home.

Later, people criticized Bjarni for not exploring the lands he had seen. Bjarni didn't care. He had wanted to find his father and kinfolk, and that is exactly what he had done, without losing his ship, his cargo, or any of his crew.

Bjarni made one more trip to Norway, where he visited Norway's ruler and told him about the lands he had seen. Then the young Icelander sailed back to Greenland and lived there as a farmer for the rest of his life.

Some time after Bjarni's arrival in Greenland, Leif also made a voyage to Norway. There are two interesting stories told about this voyage of Leif's.

The first story says that the king of Norway asked Leif to preach the Christian religion to the Greenlanders. Leif is said to have replied that this would be very hard, since his father was a devout believer in Thor, one of the old Norse gods. Before the year 1000, many people in Iceland and Greenland were followers

The Norse god Thor.

of Thor, who was believed to carry a mighty hammer with which he made thunder, calmed the sea storms, and in general protected those who were faithful to him. Thor was supposed to have red hair and a red beard and was considered especially important by seafarers.

Nevertheless, the story credits Leif with converting Greenland to Christianity. Many scholars doubt that Leif did this, believing instead that this story was made up by a monk many years after Leif's death. But at least some parts of this story seem true, the parts having to do with Leif's mother, Thjodhild.

It is said that, after Leif's voyage to Norway, Thjodhild became a Christian, and then had many arguments with Leif's father about religion. She threatened to leave Erik. To keep peace in the family, so the story goes, Erik told Thjodhild she could build a little church for herself, as long as it was out of sight of the main house and Erik didn't have to look at it.

Archaeologists have found the ruins of Thjodhild's church on Greenland. It was a tiny wood-and-turf structure, with room in it for only a few people. It was built about 200 yards (180 m) from Brattahlid, hidden behind a low hill.

We have no evidence that would tell us for sure what Leif's religious beliefs really were. But whatever they were, he could not have pleased both his Thor-loving father and his Christian mother.

The second story about Leif's voyage to Norway says that on the way his ship ran into storms. Leif and his crew were forced to take shelter in the Hebrides, islands off the mainland of Scotland that the Vikings had raided and settled long ago. There, the story goes, Leif met a woman named Thorgunna, a nobleman's daughter. Thorgunna had "unusual knowledge," meaning a knowledge of witchcraft. One day, she told Leif that she wanted to go with him when he left.

Leif asked Thorgunna if her kinsmen would mind if she came with him. Thorgunna answered that she didn't care about that, but clearly the answer was yes, they would mind.

Leif wanted no part of that. He didn't want to fight with Thorgunna's powerful family. "There are so few of us," he said.

Thorgunna then told Leif she was going to have a baby, his baby. She said she foresaw that the child would be a boy. She also hinted that this child would not prove "an asset" to Leif. Thorgunna then swore that she would send the child to Greenland when he was old enough, and warned that she might come herself "before the game was played out."

Leif gave Thorgunna presents—a gold ring, a belt of carved walrus ivory, and a cloak made of Greenland wool—and left for Norway. He would take his chances with any evil Thorgunna might send his way later. That was better than a bitter struggle with Thorgunna's family now.

Thorgunna had her baby. Later, she and the child, named Thorgils, went to Iceland, where they apparently became involved in a series of hauntings and other grim, mysterious events. Thorgunna died in Iceland, but Thorgils later went on to Greenland. Apparently Leif accepted Thorgils as his son, and the Greenlanders accepted him as a member of the community. Nevertheless, it was generally believed that there was something weird or uncanny about the man.

Maybe there is some basis to this story, and maybe not. But Leif never married, as far as we know, nor had any offspring other than Thorgils. The historical record mentions the marriage of Leif's brother, Thorstein, and the marriage of Leif's sister, Freydis. But nowhere is anything said about Leif having a wife and children. And this is the man who became Greenland's law speaker and leading citizen, a man who is described as "tall and strong, very impressive in looks, shrewd, moderate in all things, and fair-dealing."

TO VINLAND

For some fourteen or fifteen years, nothing was done about the lands Bjarni had seen to the west. During those years, the Greenland colony settled into its routines and grew.

By about the year 1000, however, some Greenlanders may have taken thought about their wood supply. Their homes and barns were built mainly of stone, but wood was needed for roof pillars and crossbeams supporting the turf roofs. Wood was also needed for benches, buckets, looms, and other household items, and for fuel for heating and cooking.

The Greenlanders had yet another use for wood. They made some iron for nails, knives, and other tools from an iron ore called bog iron. To turn this ore into iron, high temperatures were needed. Such temperatures could be achieved only in charcoal fires, and charcoal is made from wood. The Greenlanders also preferred burning charcoal in their home-fires, because it burns smokelessly.

By 1000, it may have occurred to some Greenlanders that those wooded lands Bjarni had seen might be worth checking out. It also may be that some high-spirited Greenlanders felt the need for a little excitement, if not glory.

In any case, Leif went to Bjarni in the summer of 1000 or 1001 and bought his ship. Then Leif asked his father, Erik, to lead the expedition, saying that Erik's luck would be needed on such a voyage to unknown lands. Erik said he was too old, but finally agreed. Then, as Erik was riding to the ship, his horse threw him.

Falling from one's horse at the beginning of a journey was considered a very bad omen by the Norsemen. So Erik said, "I am not meant to discover any more lands," and went back to Brattahlid.

We can be sure that Leif discussed every detail of the voyage with Bjarni. Leif meant to follow Bjarni's course in reverse. This involved sailing first to the high, glaciered, "worthless" land that Bjarni had sighted last, and then traveling south and west to the other lands Bjarni had seen.

Leif and a crew of thirty-four men sailed out of the Brattahlid fjord and then turned north, sailing up the Greenland coast past the Western Settlement. Then Leif steered northwest, toward what is now Baffin Island. After a voyage of some 600 miles (960 km), Leif and his men came upon the land Bjarni had described— a land of high glaciers and rock.

Leif and a few members of the crew went ashore in a small boat.

"At least we have done better than Bjarni," Leif said. "We have set foot on this land, anyway." Because the land between the shore and the glaciers seemed to be just one huge slab of rock, Leif called this place Helluland, which means "Slab Land" or "Flatstone Land" in Leif's language, Old Norse.

Then Leif and his party went back to the ship and sailed off in a southwesterly direction. Soon they sighted another land and again anchored the ship. Once more, Leif and a small party went ashore in the small boat. The land they found was flat, with beaches of white sand and some trees.

"This land shall be called Markland, after its resources," Leif said. Markland means "Wood Land" in Old Norse. Leif and his men were apparently not very impressed with Markland, because after the land-naming they hurried back to their ship "as fast as they could."

Leif and his men sailed on for two days, behind a wind that

*An artist's conception of Leif Erikson
about to land in North America.*

blew from the northeast. Then they sighted an island, and in back
of that a headland or cape jutting north. When they landed on the
island, they found dew on the grass and drank it. It seemed the
sweetest or freshest water they had ever tasted.

Then they went back to the ship, sailed in a westward direction between the island and the headland, and came to a very wide
area of shallow water. At low tide, the sea retreated so much that
it was almost out of sight, and their ship was left high and dry.
Leif and his men were so eager to go ashore, however, that they
took the small boat and rowed to a place where a river flowed into

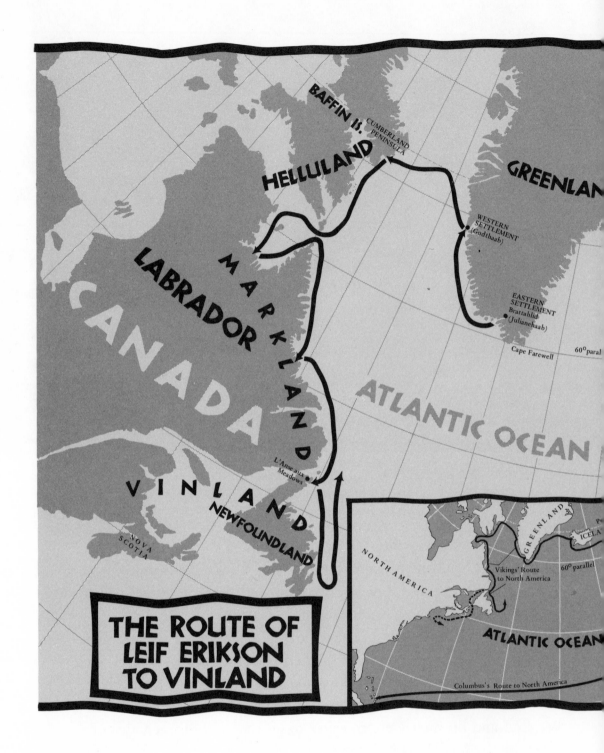

THE ROUTE OF
LEIF ERIKSON
TO VINLAND

Leif's booths.

the sea from a lake. When the tide rose again, they rowed back to the now free-floating knörr and then brought it up the river to the lake, where they anchored it.

At first, Leif had only booths built. Booths were small, temporary shelters with turf or stone walls covered with skin awnings. But Leif and his men decided to stay for the winter, and so they built at least one large house. Why did they decide to stay?

For one thing, the river and lake contained the largest salmon the Greenlanders had ever seen. Secondly, Leif and his men were greatly impressed by the rich pasture available. Words meaning "choice" or "kind" were used to describe this aspect of the country. It is said that no frost came in winter, and that the grass hardly withered, so that livestock could graze all winter and no fodder had to be cut. We don't know for certain if Leif brought cattle with him, although there are indications that he did. Furthermore, it would have been very much in character for the prudent Leif to bring an on-the-hoof supply of milk and meat with him. In any case, the two things about this land that seem to have made a favorable first impression on Leif and his crew were the salmon and the rich pasture.

In addition, there was clearly enough wood in this country for house-building.

After the house-building was finished, Leif set about exploring. He split his men into two groups. One group would remain at the camp. The other would explore, but never go so far that they couldn't get back by nightfall. All the members of the exploring group were to stay together at all times. Leif wanted to take no chances, and this caution paid off. No member of his crew got lost or came to any harm.

One day, however, a man named Tyrkir wandered off. Tyrkir was a "southerner," or German, and had been a servant in Erik's household for many years. As a child, Leif had grown very fond of Tyrkir.

Leif was furious when he heard that Tyrkir had wandered off, and dressed down his men for allowing it to happen. Although it was getting dark, Leif took twelve of his men and set off to find Tyrkir. Before they had gone very far, however, they saw Tyrkir coming toward them.

Tyrkir was acting very strangely. He was rolling his eyes, giggling, making funny faces, and babbling in German, a language that none of the Greenlanders understood.

Then Tyrkir finally spoke in Old Norse.

"I have found vines and grapes," he said.

"Is that true?" asked Leif.

"Where I was born, there were plenty of vines and grapes," Tyrkir answered.

This is probably the most famous episode in all the stories told about Leif and the new land he explored. It may also be one of the few episodes that is completely misleading.

Many people assume that Tyrkir's giggling and silly behavior means that he was drunk. But it is very unlikely that Tyrkir could have gotten drunk just by eating grapes. Grapes do not turn alcoholic on the vine. If grapes are picked and left lying around, they either rot or—in certain hot, dry climates—turn into raisins. If grapes are crushed, the result is grape juice, not wine. Turning grape juice into wine takes not only time but also certain ingredients that Tyrkir almost certainly did not have.

If it is unlikely that Tyrkir got drunk on grapes, what could have caused his strange behavior? It is possible that what Tyrkir really found was a plant called vetch, a member of the pea and bean family. Several kinds of vetch have creeping, vinelike stalks and a pealike fruit. Vetch grows in many places in continental Europe—where Tyrkir may have encountered it before—and in North America. Several kinds can be eaten by people, and many other kinds are used for animal feed. Sometimes, when the soil is acid, some kinds of vetch turn into locoweed. Locoweed gets its name from the effect it has on livestock—it makes them "loco," or crazy.

The episode of the grapes has other peculiar aspects. For example, the morning after Tyrkir was found, Leif said this to his men: "Now we have two jobs to do. First, we have to cut wood. Then we have to gather grapes *or* cut vines."

It sounds almost as though the person who wrote down this episode wasn't sure what Leif told his men, and offered "gather grapes" *or* "cut vines" as two possible explanations of a combination of words that otherwise made no sense to him. It is said that Leif wanted his men to "gather grapes" or "cut vines" so that he would have cargo for his ship. But would grapes or vines have been a *valuable* cargo?

We must remember that Leif and the other Greenlanders had probably never seen real grapes or grapevines. Grapes never grew in Iceland or Greenland. Norsemen were unfamiliar with wine or wine-making techniques. Of what value would grapes have been to Greenlanders? Some people have suggested that vines could be used for making cables or ropes. But we know that the Greenlanders made and exported a rope of walrus hide so strong that sixty men pulling on it couldn't break it. We never hear of Greenlanders exporting or otherwise using vines.

In any case, the story says that Leif's men cut wood and gathered grapes or cut vines on alternate days, until the ship had a full cargo of wood and the small boat was filled with grapes.

After these jobs were done, Leif and his men settled in for the winter. They observed that winter days and nights were of more equal length in this country than in Greenland or Iceland. On the shortest day, sunup was at nine in the morning, and sundown was at three in the afternoon.

When spring came, Leif and his men prepared to leave. Just before they were ready to go, Leif gave this new country a name. The name, Leif said, was chosen to describe the land "and the good things found in it." The name Leif chose was Vinland.

But what exactly does *Vin*land mean? There are two separate *vin* words in Old Norse. One, *vín*, written with an accent, means "wine." This word was rarely used in Icelandic Old Norse even during the 1300s and 1400s, and it did not start being used at all until after 1000. The other *vin*, without an accent, was a very ancient Norse word. People stopped using it, at least in writing, before 1000. This *vin* meant "pasture" or "meadow." Thus the name Leif chose could have meant either "Pastureland" or "Wineland."

For a long time, people assumed it meant Wineland, but today we aren't sure.

When Leif and his men left the newly named Vinland, they took with them a full shipload of wood and the ship's boat full of "grapes." We should keep two things in mind here. First, there is nothing in the stories to suggest that the wood Leif took from Vinland was cut from *large* trees. Most Greenlanders or Icelanders had probably never seen a large tree. If large trees existed in Vinland, Leif's men surely would have mentioned it, just as they mentioned the extra-large salmon. We must assume, therefore, that the trees Leif's men cut down were similar in height and thickness to those found in their Greenland home.

Secondly, there is that boatload of "grapes." These grapes had been picked and loaded the previous summer. It is difficult to imagine Leif towing back a boatload of rotten grapes. If, however, these "grapes" were actually dried-out pealike or beanlike legumes, they might have had value as food, either for people or for livestock.

The voyage back to Greenland went well, with clear sailing all the way. Before long, the mountains and glaciers of Greenland came into view.

Then one of the crew asked Leif why he was steering so close to the wind. This meant that Leif was pointing the ship almost directly into the wind, a very tricky thing to do, especially with the single square sail of the Viking knörr.

Leif tartly replied that he was keeping his eye on his steering. But he was also watching something in the distance, maybe a reef or a ship. Did anyone else see it?

Nobody did.

Leif could now make out a reef in the distance and saw that there were people on it. He then explained why he was steering so close to the wind. By doing so, he could approach the reef very

Leif was a sharp-eyed and alert seaman.

slowly, since the wind was almost blowing the ship backwards. He could see if the people on the reef needed help. But if the people proved hostile, Leif could turn the ship quickly and catch the wind at an angle that would carry it swiftly out of danger.

The people on the reef—fifteen in all—had been shipwrecked there. They were led by a man named Thorir.

Leif took all the strangers on board. He also let them take with them as many of their possessions as his ship had room for. When the ship reached Greenland, Leif took some of Thorir's group to Brattahlid and found other homes for the rest.

Because he saved these people, and because his voyage to Vinland was a success, Leif was given the nickname Leif the Lucky.

In the winter of the year Leif returned to Greenland, Erik the Red died. Thus Leif inherited Brattahlid and the leadership of the Greenland colony. Also during that winter, Thorir and most of the shipwreck survivors became ill and died. The following spring, Leif sent a ship to pick up a cargo of timber that Thorir had had to abandon on the reef. Leif never missed an opportunity to add to his wealth.

As the new law speaker and leader of the Eastern Settlement, Leif's exploring days were over. Others would have to take up the challenge of Vinland, if they chose to. And others did choose to, especially other members of Leif's family.

VINLAND REVISITED

The next visitor to Vinland was Leif's brother Thorvald.

While exploring a headland or cape to the north and east of Vinland, Thorvald and a small party of men came upon a deep fjord.

"This is a lovely place," Thorvald said. "I will make my home here someday."

Then, for the first time, Greenlanders saw Indians. There were nine of them, asleep under their skin boats. For some reason, Thorvald decided to attack. He and his men killed eight of the Indians, but the ninth escaped.

The next day, a whole fleet of Indians in skin boats attacked Thorvald's party. During the fight, Thorvald was struck by an arrow. It entered his body through the armpit. Thorvald pulled the arrow out himself, and said, "Here it is. It will be my death. Bury me here, and put crosses at my head and feet. Call this place Krossaness ["the Cape of the Crosses"] from now on. I seem to have spoken truth when I said I would settle here for a while." Then he died.

Thorvald's men buried him as he had asked, and then rejoined the main group at Leif's houses in Vinland. They stayed there over the winter, and returned to Greenland the following spring with a cargo of "grapes" and "vines."

Leif now had one brother left, Thorstein. Thorstein decided to go to Vinland and bring back Thorvald's body. But Thorstein's

The wounding of Thorvald.

Thorfinn and Gudrid in the New World.

ship ran into violent summer storms and was knocked back and forth within the Davis Strait. Thorstein finally brought his ship to harbor in the Western Settlement, just as winter began. Worn out and weakened, Thorstein and many of his crew became ill. Thorstein died before the winter was over.

Thus Leif lost both his brothers, both in connection with voyages to Vinland.

Some years later, a wealthy Icelander named Thorfinn Karlsefni visited Greenland. After talking with Leif, Karlsefni decided that he wanted to go to Vinland. He asked if he could have Leif's houses there. Leif said no, but Karlsefni could *borrow* the houses if he wished. Karlsefni gathered 160 people, including women, for his voyage to Vinland.

But here the stories get very confused. Today, we are not sure that Karlsefni ever found the place that Leif called Vinland. Karlsefni's expedition definitely arrived *somewhere* in North America and stayed there for three years. Karlsefni's wife, Gudrid, had a son there named Snorri, the first white child known to have been born in North America. During his three-year stay, Karlsefni traded with the Indians and gained many valuable furs. After a while, however, trouble developed with the Indians, who began to attack Karlsefni's colony. He finally decided to leave when it became clear that his relatively small colony could never survive the repeated and massive Indian attacks. So, in about 1013, Karlsefni returned to Greenland, his ship richly laden with furs and timber. After that, he and his wife sailed to Iceland and made their home there.

More than 200 years later, when the stories about Greenland and Vinland were written down, they were written by descendants of Karlsefni and Gudrid and by others who had reason to respect this important Icelandic family.

Excited by the rich cargo of wood and furs that Karlsefni had brought back, Leif's sister, Freydis, announced that she too wanted to visit Vinland. Could *she* have the Vinland houses? she asked Leif. No, he told her, but she could borrow them, just like Karlsefni.

Freydis organized an expedition of two ships. The larger of the two was owned by two brothers from Iceland, Helgi and Finnbogi. Freydis owned the other ship. It was agreed that all members of the expedition would share equally in the profits of the voyage. It was also agreed that each ship would carry the same number of able-bodied men—thirty. But Freydis broke this agreement and smuggled an extra five men aboard her ship. Apparently she wanted her group to be the stronger in case of trouble with Helgi and Finnbogi, and may already have been planning to harm them.

The expedition reached Vinland safely; but soon after its arrival, Freydis began to quarrel with Helgi and Finnbogi. She refused to share Leif's houses with the brothers and their group. As a result, Helgi and Finnbogi built a house farther inland, near a lake. During the winter, there were more quarrels between the two groups.

Very early one spring morning, Freydis went to see Finnbogi in his house near the lake. She woke Finnbogi up and asked him if he would exchange ships with her, saying she wanted to leave Vinland. Freydis now had a large store of timber and wanted the larger ship because it would hold more. Finnbogi agreed, thinking that this generous act would ease the tensions between the two groups. Besides, both groups were going to share equally in the total profits, so it didn't matter if one ship carried more cargo than the other. Then Finnbogi went back to bed.

Freydis returned to Leif's houses and woke up her men. She told them that the brothers had beaten her up after she had offered to buy their ship. She demanded that her men avenge this insult, and taunted them until they agreed to do so. Then Freydis and her men went to the brothers' house. The people there were still asleep. Freydis's men seized the people in the house and tied them up. Freydis then had each of Helgi and Finnbogi's men brought outside, one by one, and killed.

There were also five women in the brothers' group. But Freydis's men refused to kill the women.

Then Freydis said, "Give me an ax." She was handed an ax, and with it she chopped the five women to death.

Freydis, using a combination of threats and bribes, got her men to promise that they wouldn't tell the truth about what had happened. They would say instead that the thirty-five murdered people had decided to stay in Vinland.

Soon afterward, Freydis and her crew returned to Greenland, using the larger ship. Freydis went home to her farm in Gardar, very pleased with herself. Before long, however, some members of Freydis's crew began to talk. When rumors about what had really happened reached Leif, he was horrified. He tortured three members of Freydis's crew to find out if the rumors were true. They were.

Then Leif said, "I do not have the heart to punish my sister as she deserves. All I can say is that she and her family will never prosper."

From then on, we are told, the Greenlanders despised Freydis.

But how did the Greenlanders feel about Leif? The punishment Freydis deserved was death, and, as law speaker, Leif had a duty to say this. He didn't, and instead pronounced a curse on Freydis and her family.

We don't know if Leif meant to include himself when he said that Freydis *and her family* would never prosper. Whether he meant to or not, this is the last time that the name of Leif Erikson appears in any of the Old Norse stories about Greenland and Vinland. The stories are strangely silent about the time and manner of Leif's death. It is mentioned that some people visited Greenland in 1025 and found that Thorgils was now the leader in Brattahlid, but that is all. After 1025, Leif and all the Erikson family seem to disappear completely from the historical record. And never again does anyone claim descent from Leif Erikson.

Markland and Vinland, the names Leif gave to the places he visited, did not fade away, however. They are mentioned in Icelandic records again and again. They are often mentioned in a very casual way, suggesting that many people in Greenland and Iceland knew exactly where these places were. But this knowledge has been lost, and today we aren't sure where Leif's Markland and Vinland are.

WHERE IS
VINLAND?

There are two main written accounts of early Greenland and the Vinland voyages—the *Greenlanders' Saga* and *Erik the Red's Saga*. *Saga* is an Old Norse word meaning "a telling." The *Greenlanders' Saga* was written in Iceland sometime before 1200, or almost 200 years after the events it describes. *Erik's Saga* was written in about 1260, also in Iceland. The original documents have been lost, but copies based on them appear in Icelandic books written in the 1300s and 1400s.

Both the sagas probably began as family histories—stories told in Greenland and Iceland as entertainment and as a way of teaching. But the versions we have today are not hearth-fire folktales. The sagas are written books, composed by learned men in Iceland at a time when Iceland was becoming one of Europe's important centers of scholarship and literature.

Most of the people who wrote or worked on the sagas were churchmen. Many of them had been educated in Europe and knew Latin, the language in which most knowledge available to learned Europeans was stored.

Sometimes the saga writers checked with people who had heard something from their grandparents, who had in turn heard something from someone who had actually lived during Erik's or Leif's time. But most of the time, the saga writers got their information from books. As a result, sometimes they added things to

A page from the Flatey Book, *a collection of Norse sagas and poems, compiled between 1387 and 1395. This book gives a lengthy version of the Vinland episode.*

the sagas that came from their own time, not from the time of Erik or Leif. For example, in *Erik's Saga* it is written that Leif's brother Thorvald was shot with an arrow by a uniped, a mythical one-legged creature. Unipeds were supposed to live in Africa. Where did this uniped idea come from?

Almost all learned northern Europeans of the 1300s and 1400s believed that there was only one huge continent, and that this land circled the northern half of the globe. They also believed that Vinland was probably the back end of Africa, which they thought reached all the way around the globe from the east.

Actually, these scholars were not all that wrong. Most of the earth's landmass *is* north of the equator. If the frozen north polar regions are considered land, rather than water, most of the earth's landmass *is* connected together.

The idea of a single landmass, with Vinland being the back, or western, side of Africa, lingered in Iceland throughout the 1400s, even after Greenland had been cut off by ice packs from any contact with Iceland or Europe. This idea may even have had something to do with Columbus's discovery of Central America.

In Columbus's time, scholars in Portugal and Spain knew that the earth was round and that it was about 25,000 miles (40,230 km) wide around the equator. Most of them did not know, however, that the American landmass stood between Europe and Asia to the west. They said, rightly, that the "Indies"—Japan and China —had to be about 12,000 miles (19,300 km) westward from Europe. No one in Columbus's time could make a 12,000-mile ocean voyage without stopping for water and food—the crew would die.

But Columbus *insisted* that the Indies were only about 2,500 miles (4,000 km) to the west. He was so sure of his calculations that he was able to convince people in Spain to finance his voyage. In 1492, Columbus encountered land almost exactly when and where he said he would. He believed that this land—Central America—was the Indies. But where did Columbus get his conviction that he would strike land only 2,500 miles (4,000 km) across the Atlantic?

Columbus is said to have visited Iceland in his youth. Whether he did or not, he almost certainly knew about the stories of Leif's Vinland and the idea that Vinland was a part of Africa. Columbus may have decided that the Icelanders were wrong to believe that "Wineland" was Africa, and he may have concluded that Leif had really explored the outlying parts of the "Indies." After all, the sagas described the "Wineland" natives as dark-haired, high-cheekboned, almond-eyed, and short. And it was known that Asians had similar features.

In any case, Columbus was absolutely certain that the Hispanic scholars of his time had somehow made a mistake, and that the world was either much narrower than they said, or that Asia was much bigger and closer to southern Europe than they believed. It is likely that the sagas about Vinland at least *added* to Columbus's conviction about this. And so there may be a tiny, almost invisible thread leading from Leif's exploration of Vinland to Columbus's discovery of Central America almost five centuries later.

The "vines" and "grapes" of the sagas may be another example of something added by the saga writers. The earliest known mention of Vinland in Western Europe occurs in a book written in Latin in about 1075 by a German named Adam of Bremen. Adam wrote that Vinland was an island "called Wineland from the circumstance that vines grow there of their own accord and produce the most excellent wine," and said he got that information from a Danish king. Adam, and the Icelandic saga-writers who later read his book, may have thought that the antique Norse word *vin* was the same as the brand-new Norse word *vín*, "wine," borrowed from the Latin word *vinum*. But the Icelandic saga-writers

adbuiat. descendens sau ad hiemale solsticiu. simul
tbe fac austlib? ls ignorantes pagani. tra illa uo
cant scam. beata q tale miracln pster mortalib?
taq; rex danou e multis alus testat~ li ibi tng
sic in suedia i noruegia q i ectis q ibi st insulis.
Preterea una adhuc regione recitauit a multis e
eo repta oceano q dr winland. eo qd ibi uites spo
te nascant uinu optimu ferentes. sta fruges ibi
ñ seminatas habundare ñ fabulosa opinione s; et
opim relatione danou. Ite nob retulit be
memorie pontifex adalbt in dieb an decessouis s
qsda nobiles de frisia uitos cu puagandi maris i
boreã uela retendisse. eo qd ab incolis eu ipsi dr ab
ostio wurahe flum. directo csu i aqlone nulla e
ta ocrere pr infinitu oceanu. Cui rei nouitate
p uestiganda. iuuati sodales a littore frisonu leto

Adam of Breman's Historia.
The page shown contains the first recorded
reference (7th line) to Vinland (Winland).

also knew that there was no "excellent wine" to be had in Greenland or Iceland. So the saga writers had a problem. Adam of Bremen said that Vinland had grapes and vines. But they knew personally that no wine had ever come out of Greenland, which resembled Iceland in climate. So they may have tried to solve this problem by making Vinland sound warmer and more likely to have grapes than it really was.

Parts of the *Greenlanders' Saga* and *Erik's Saga* sharply contradict each other. Many scholars today agree, however, that the *Greenlanders' Saga* is probably more accurate about the voyages of Erik, Bjarni, and Leif. They also believe that *Erik's Saga* probably contains accurate details about several different places in North America. From 1000 to at least 1200, Greenlanders made many trips to the nearby parts of North America. It is almost certain that bits and pieces of information about these different North American voyages found their way into *Erik's Saga*. Other parts of *Erik's Saga*, like the mention of Thjodhild's church, were either unknown to the writers of the earlier *Greenlanders' Saga* or were considered unimportant.

But, with all their contradictions and possible inaccuracies, the two sagas have proved right about most things. For a long time, modern people weren't even sure that Norse colonies had really existed on *Greenland*, to say nothing about Vinland. But in the 1920s, Danish archaeologists, using the sagas as a guide, began digging in the Julianehaab area and started turning up Norse home-sites, including the Brattahlid of Erik and Leif.

Until recently, most people believed that Vinland was to be found in what is now the United States. They were led to this belief mainly because of the grapes mentioned in the sagas. Today, grapes don't grow much farther north than southern New England. So most people looked for Vinland in the Cape Cod area, or farther south—in New York, Virginia, or even Florida. But some who carefully read the sagas doubted that Vinland could be that far from Greenland. The sailing directions in the sagas do *not* describe a voyage 2,000 miles (3,200 km) long, which is the sailing distance from southern Greenland to southern New England.

In addition, most people forgot that the Northmen were just that—people of the *north*. Iceland, where people have lived for at least 1,100 years, lies just south of the Arctic Circle. The Norse-inhabited parts of Greenland lay between the 60° north and 65° north parallels, in about the same belt of latitude where today most people in Norway, Sweden, Iceland, and Alaska live.

In 1960, a Norwegian named Helge Ingstad decided to forget about the "grapes." He looked farther north, in Canada, for Leif's Vinland. Near a place called L'Anse aux Meadows, on the northern tip of Newfoundland, Dr. Ingstad found the remains of a large Norse settlement.

The ruins at L'Anse aux Meadows have been carefully dug up. They look like the Norse home-sites on Greenland. One of the houses is very large, about 55 feet (16.5 m) wide by about 70 feet (21 m) long. There are also other structures, including typical Norse boat-sheds, smaller houses, cooking pits, and a smithy for making bog iron. Perhaps most interesting of all, a Norse spindle whorl was found near the main house. Norse spindle whorls were doughnut-like rings of soft stone attached to the bottom of a loom, to hold the vertical threads straight while cloth was being woven. Since weaving cloth was women's work among the Norse, we can reasonably assume that women lived at L'Anse aux Meadows, and that they lived there long enough to make cloth-weaving necessary. We know from the sagas that Thorfinn Karlsefni's expedition included women, that it stayed for three years, and that Karlsefni traded cloth with the Indians for furs.

The site at L'Anse aux Meadows fits a number of the sailing

directions and other descriptions given in the *Greenlanders' Saga*. It juts out northward into the ocean. It is south of the two landmarks named Helluland and Markland. It has lush pastures. It has a small pond, with a brook running from it into the sea. There are salmon in the brook. At low tide, the sea to the north becomes very shallow. And, according to scientific dating techniques, the site is about a thousand years old. But is L'Anse aux Meadows actually *Leif's* Vinland?

Recently, Canadian archaeologists have discovered ruins of Norse origin in several places along the west coast of Ungava Bay, in northern Quebec. Most of these sites have not been carefully dug up yet, but there are enough of them to suggest that Greenlanders made frequent visits to this area. The Ungava Bay sites are farther north than L'Anse aux Meadows, and closer to Greenland. Could one of these sites also be the place that Leif named Vinland?

In order to answer this question, we must look again at the sailing directions given in the *Greenlanders' Saga*. According to the saga, Vinland was south of two landmarks, Helluland and Markland. But do we really know where these places are?

The landmark Helluland is usually identified as Baffin Island. But Baffin Island is quite large—about 400 miles (645 km) along its eastern coast. It is unlikely that Norse sailors would use the *entire* island, rather than just some part of it, as a landmark.

Only one part of Baffin Island seems to fit the actual saga description of Helluland. This is the large tongue of land, called the Cumberland Peninsula, that juts eastward into the Davis Strait along the Arctic Circle. The Cumberland Peninsula is the only part of Baffin Island that has large glaciers visible all year round from the sea.

If Helluland is actually the Cumberland Peninsula, and not *all* of Baffin Island, where then is Markland? Many people believe that Markland—"Woodland"—is Labrador, especially the part of Labrador where great spruce forests grow. This forested region of Labrador begins about 600 miles (960 km) south of the Cumberland Peninsula, near the modern town of Nain. From there, it is about 400 miles (645 km) southwest to the tip of Newfoundland and L'Anse aux Meadows. If L'Anse aux Meadows is actually Leif's Vinland, we *have* to locate Markland in the Labrador forests.

The *Greenlanders' Saga* tells us, however, that Leif went ashore at Markland, named the place, and then left in a hurry. It is hard to imagine Leif and his men coming upon a land of towering spruce trees and not becoming hugely excited. The Greenlanders were pleased enough with their sparse, scrubby trees to call them a forest. What then would they call a *real* forest? It is hard to think why, if Markland was in fact the forests of Labrador, Markland did not become a main *destination* for the wood-hungry Greenlanders, instead of just a landmark to be used to get to Vinland. Thus, although Markland could be Labrador, there are reasons to believe it may not be.

But suppose we consider Markland to be another part of Baffin Island, a part that had *some* arctic tree and shrub growth on it? According to one writer, James Robert Enterline, there are several parts of Baffin Island where a few groves of stunted arctic trees stand out in a startling way, in an otherwise barren landscape. Such trees are unusual enough to have served as a landmark, and yet the land itself is one that nobody would particularly want to remain in. If we locate Markland as being somewhere in the southern part of Baffin Island, the Norse sites in the Ungava Bay region are then both south and west of Helluland and Markland.

If we call the western coast of Ungava Bay a possible location for Leif's Vinland, this also helps solve another puzzle in the Vinland sailing directions. Why, if Vinland was L'Anse aux Meadows, would the Cumberland Peninsula, at the Arctic Circle, be kept as a landmark? Why sail *north* and west, when all of Labrador and Newfoundland lie *south* and west of the Eastern Settlement? Using Helluland and a not-otherwise-interesting Markland as landmarks makes some sense, however, if we assume that the Greenlanders wanted to make sure that they did not sail *past* the relatively narrow entrance to Ungava Bay.

The Ungava Bay sites also fit some of the saga descriptions of Vinland. There are several places having fabulous meadows of lichen and moss. There are extensive shallows, and so forth. And, unlike L'Anse aux Meadows, there are at least two places where a knörr could be rowed or towed into a lake or lakelike basin.

So where is Leif's Vinland?

If we judge by the *Greenlanders' Saga*, and by the Norse ruins found so far, Vinland could be either L'Anse aux Meadows *or* somewhere in Ungava Bay. But it can't be both—these two locations are about 800 miles (1,280 km) apart. What would help us to pin down Vinland as being one or the other?

The *Greenlanders' Saga* tells us about two events that happened in or near Vinland. Both these events happened during Leif's lifetime, and both probably caused him sorrow and pain.

Someday, perhaps, archaeologists will find Krossaness, the burial place of Leif's brother Thorvald. This grave ought to contain a sword, spearheads, or other long-lasting grave-goods often buried with an important Northman. Perhaps it will even contain stone or metal crosses. If this grave-site is found near L'Anse aux Meadows, such a find would eliminate Ungava Bay. If Krossaness is found near Ungava Bay, it will cast a huge shadow of doubt on L'Anse aux Meadows as the site of Vinland.

The other clue to the location of Leif's Vinland might also be a burial site. Near one of the Norse sites, archaeologists may

*Leif Erikson immortalized by the great
American sculptor Alexander Calder.*

someday find some thousand-year-old signs of mass murder—perhaps a shallow, hastily dug pit big enough for thirty-five bodies and maybe a few jumbled possessions. Perhaps even a few fragments of shattered bone will remain, as another sign that Freydis was once at work here.

A NOTE ON
SOURCES

The sagas relating to the Norse adventure in the New World are to be found in Gwyn Jones' *The Norse Atlantic Saga: Being the Norse Voyages of Discovery and Settlement to Iceland, Greenland, America*, and in *The Vinland Sagas: The Norse Discovery of America*, translated with an introduction by Magnus Magnusson and Hermann Pálsson. Useful general sources are *A History of the Vikings*, by Gwyn Jones, and *The Viking Achievement*, by P. G. Foote and D. M. Wilson. In *Westward to Vinland*, Helge Ingstad describes his discoveries at L'Anse aux Meadows, and in *Viking America: The Norse Crossings and Their Legacy*, James Robert Enterline presents several riveting findings and speculations about Vinland and the Norse presence in arctic North America.

INDEX

ABOUT THE
AUTHOR

Malcolm C. Jensen has been a text-book editor for a number of years. He is the author of *America in Time*, a general reference book, and *Francisco Coronado*, another in the Visual Biography series. Mr. Jensen lives in New York.